Coloring book

This book is a coloring book for kids between the ages of 2 and 8 years

The content of this book is coloring pictures of funny animals and this is for the little boy to reveal the animals and learn and all that with a little fun

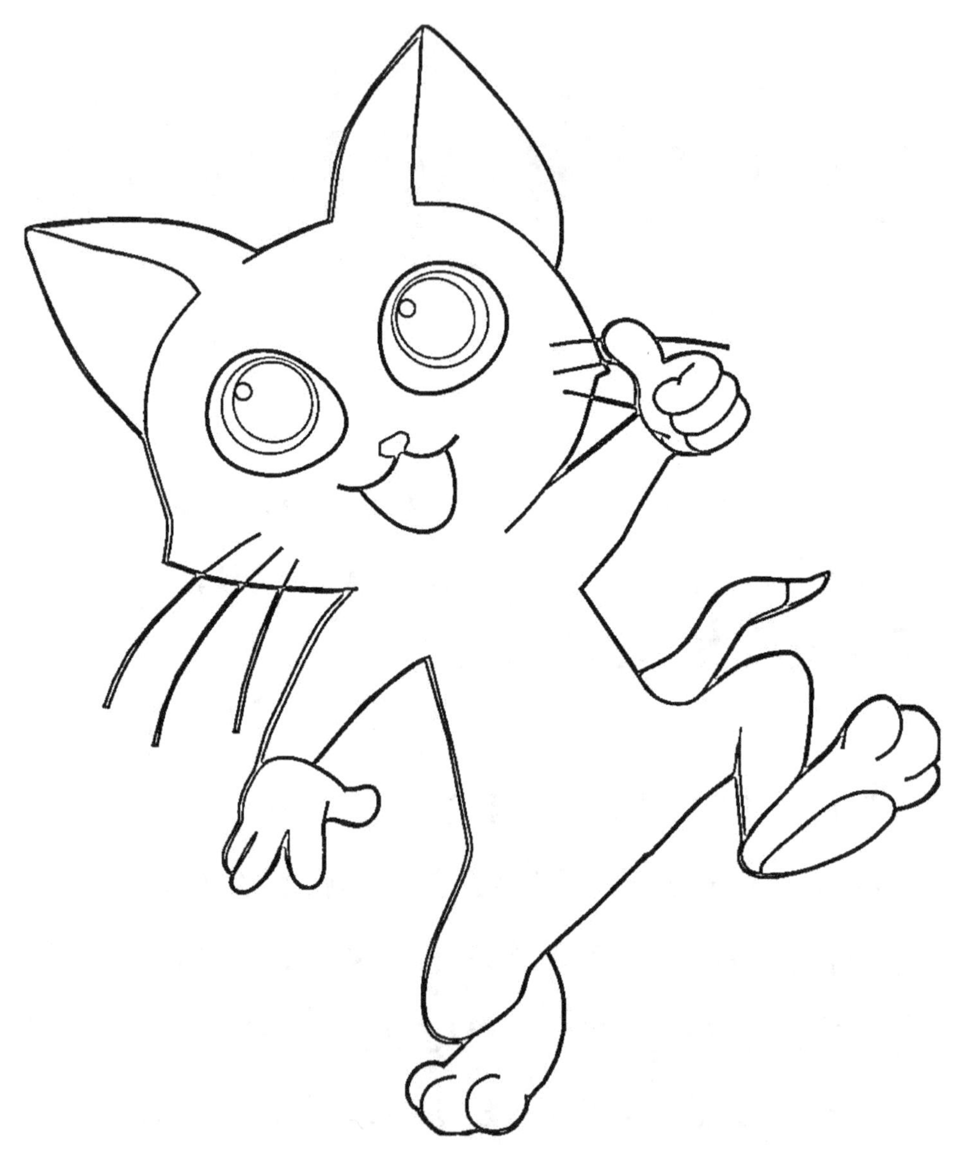

Cat

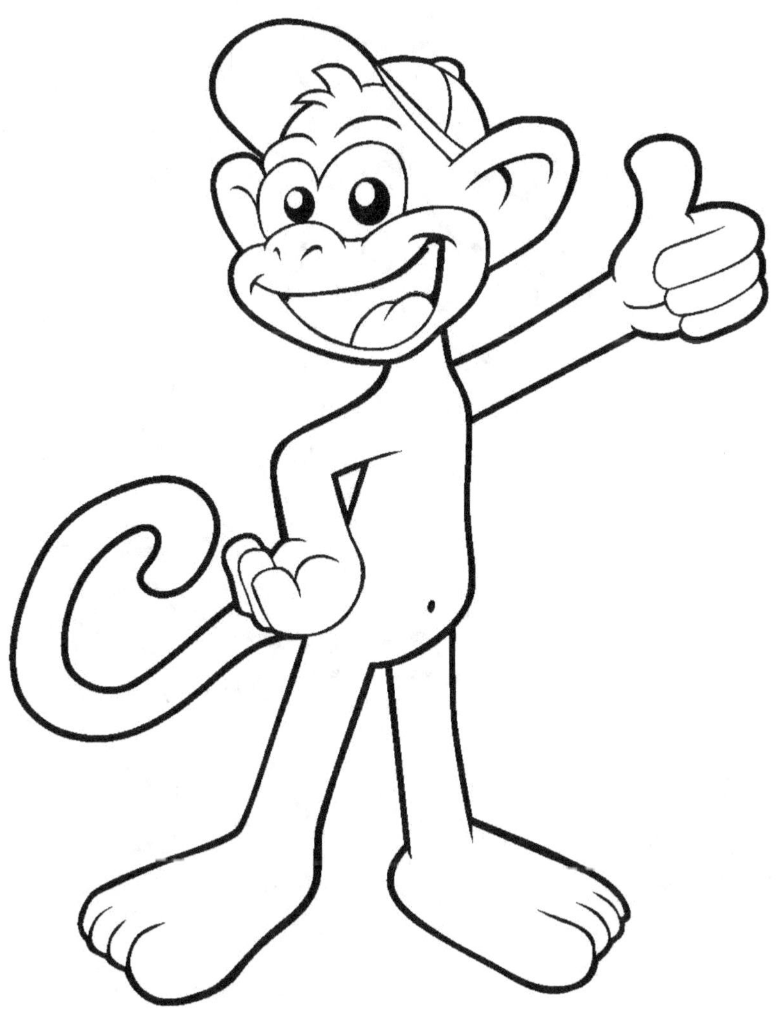

Monkey

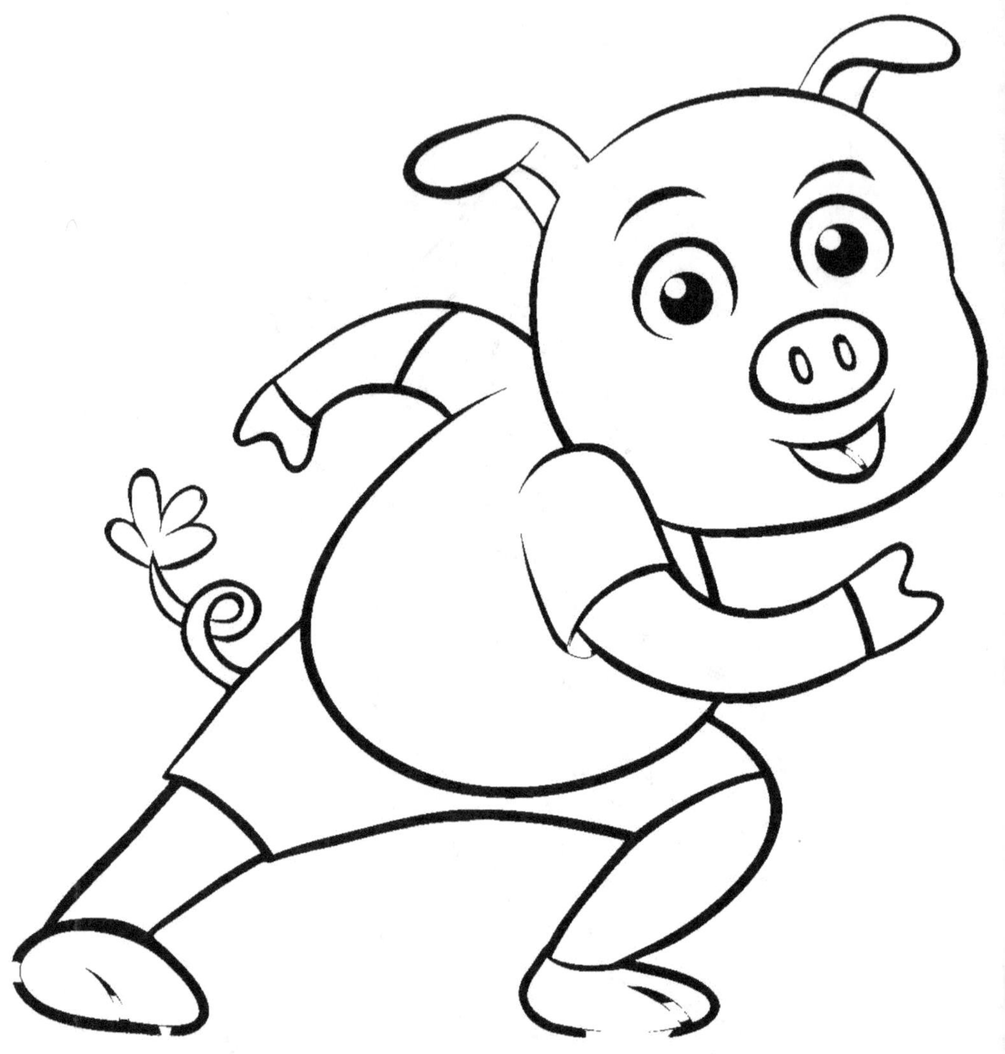

Pig

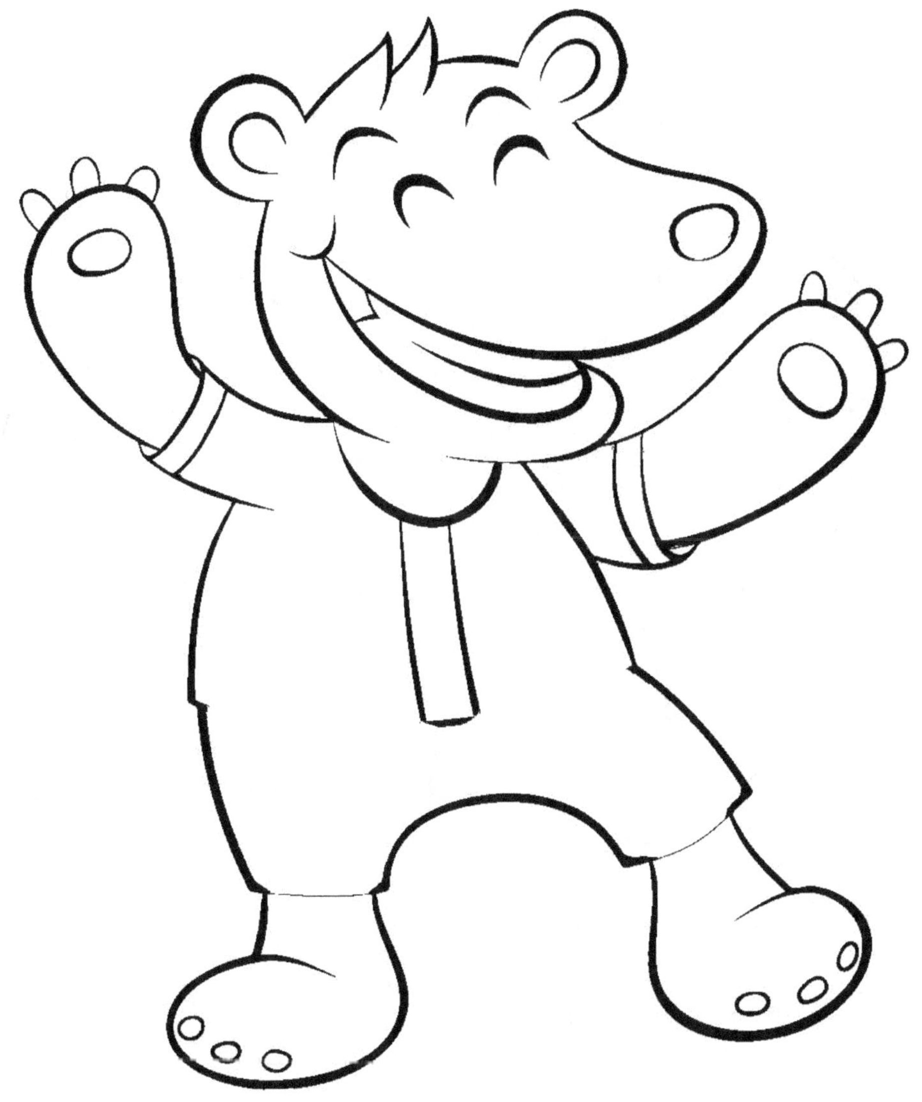

Bear

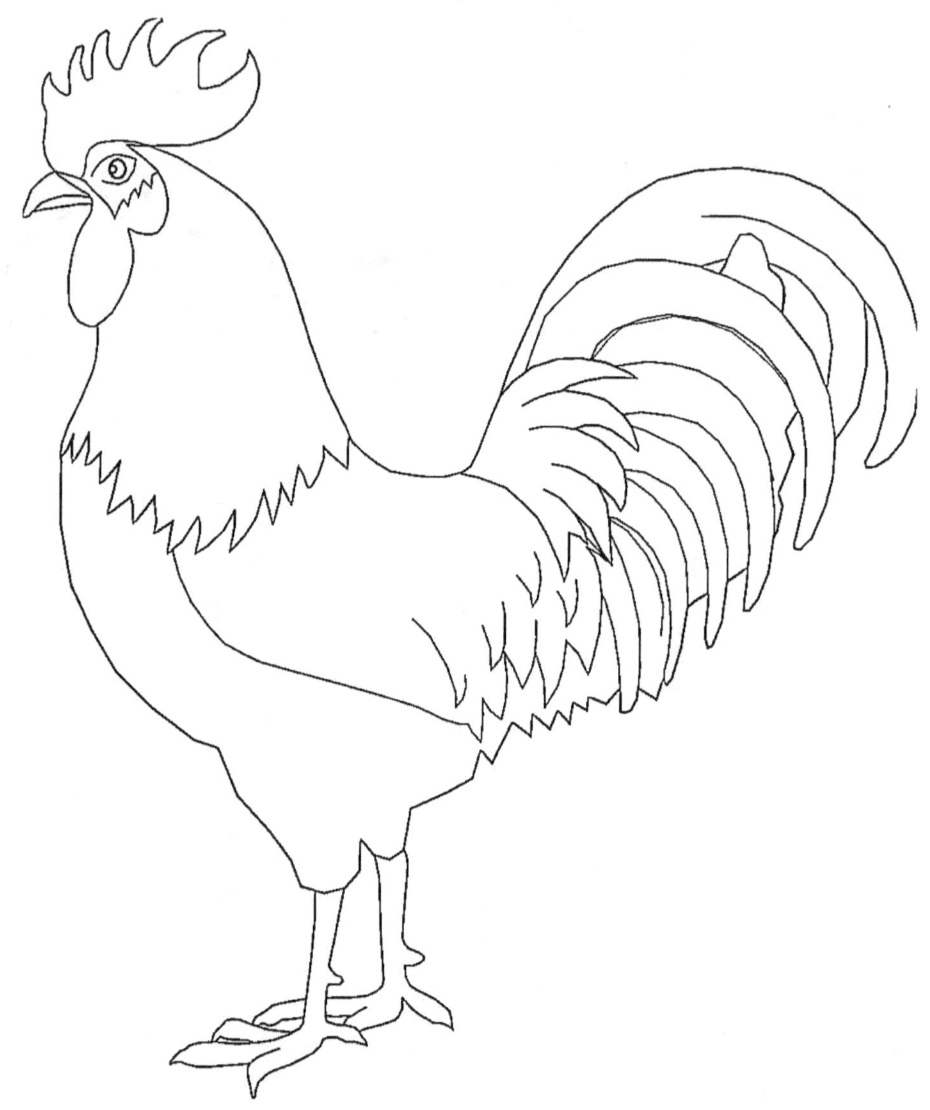

rooster

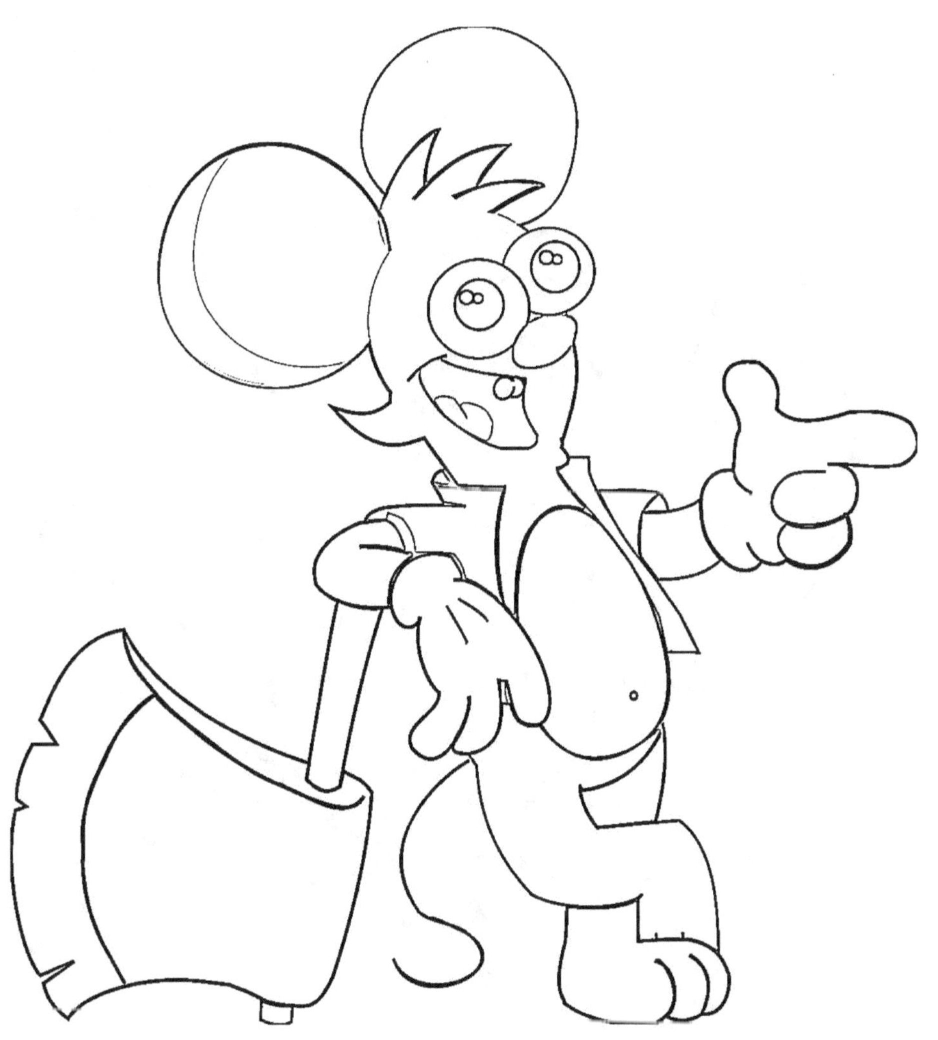

Mouse

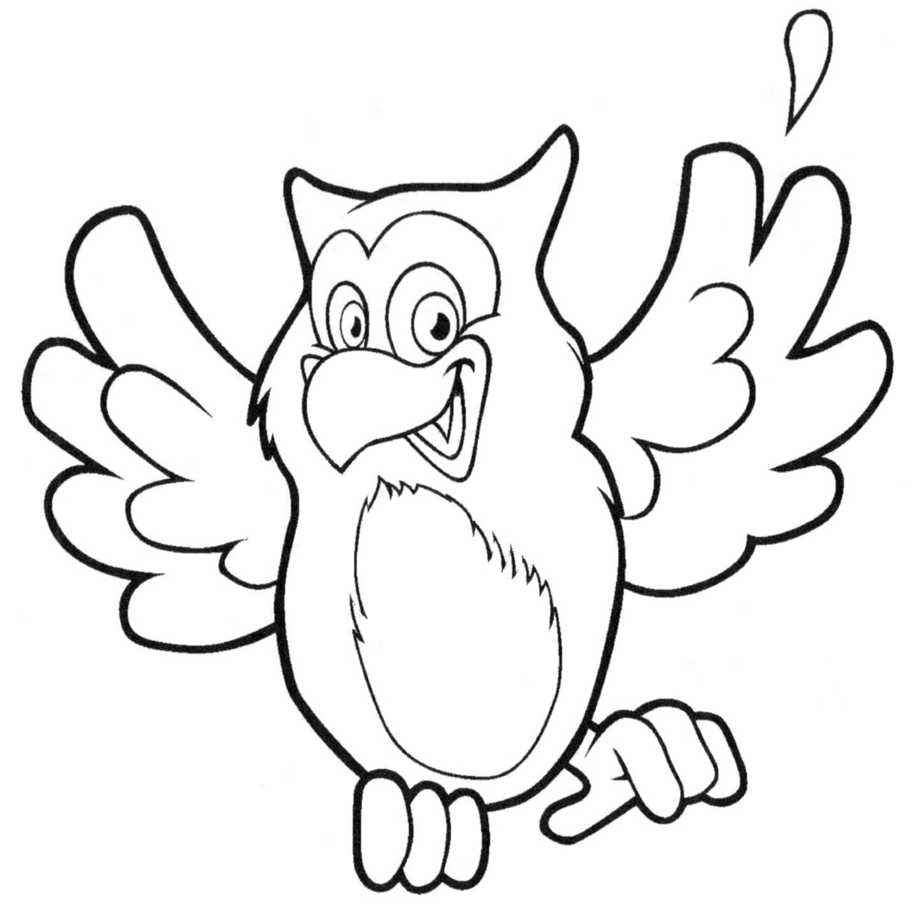

bird

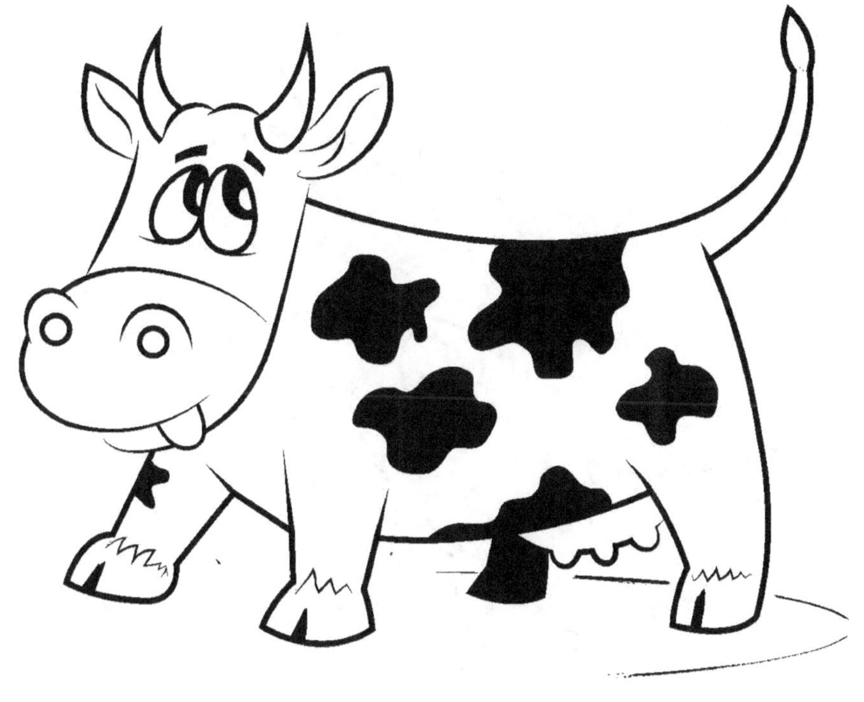

a cow

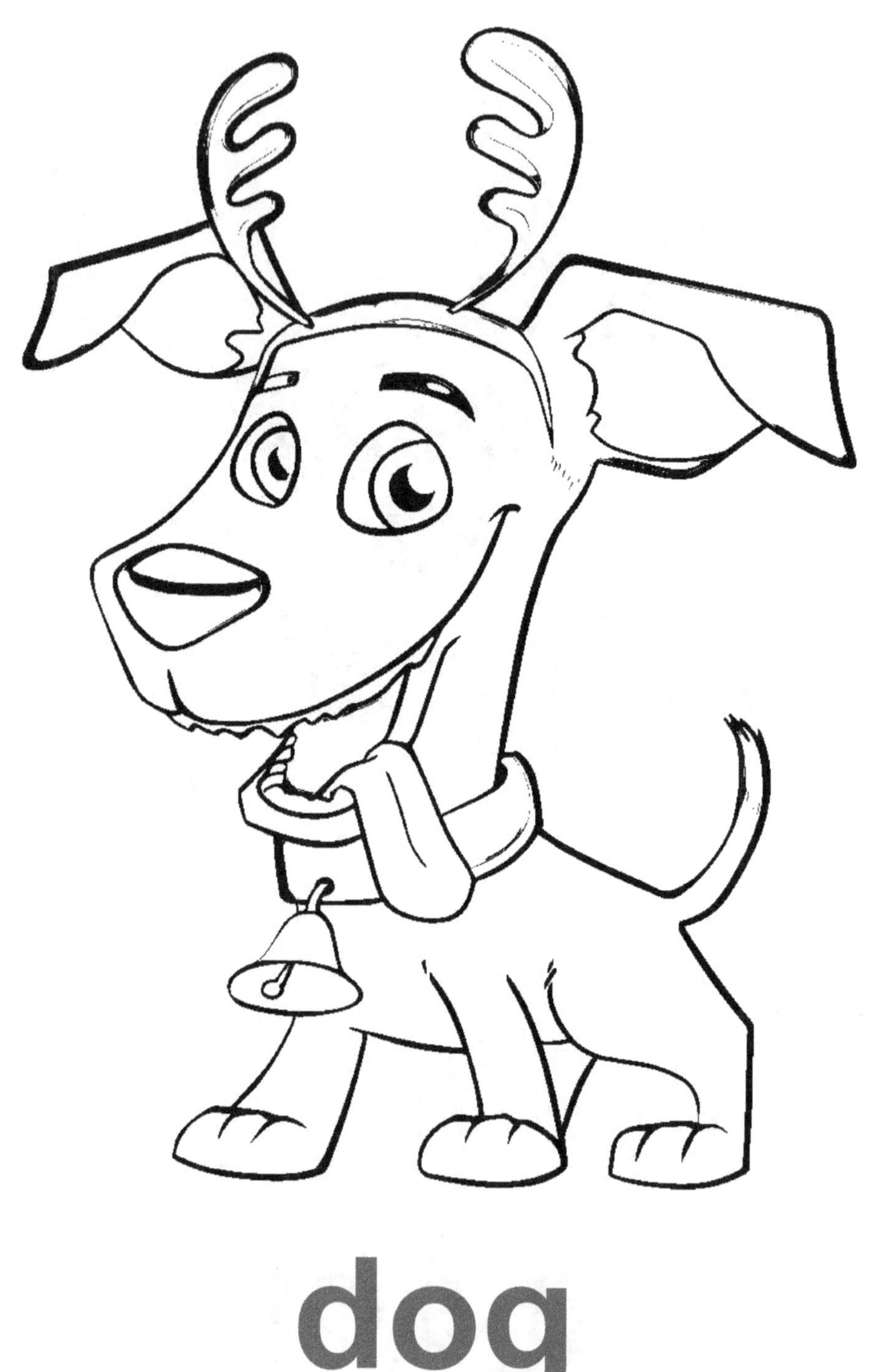

dog

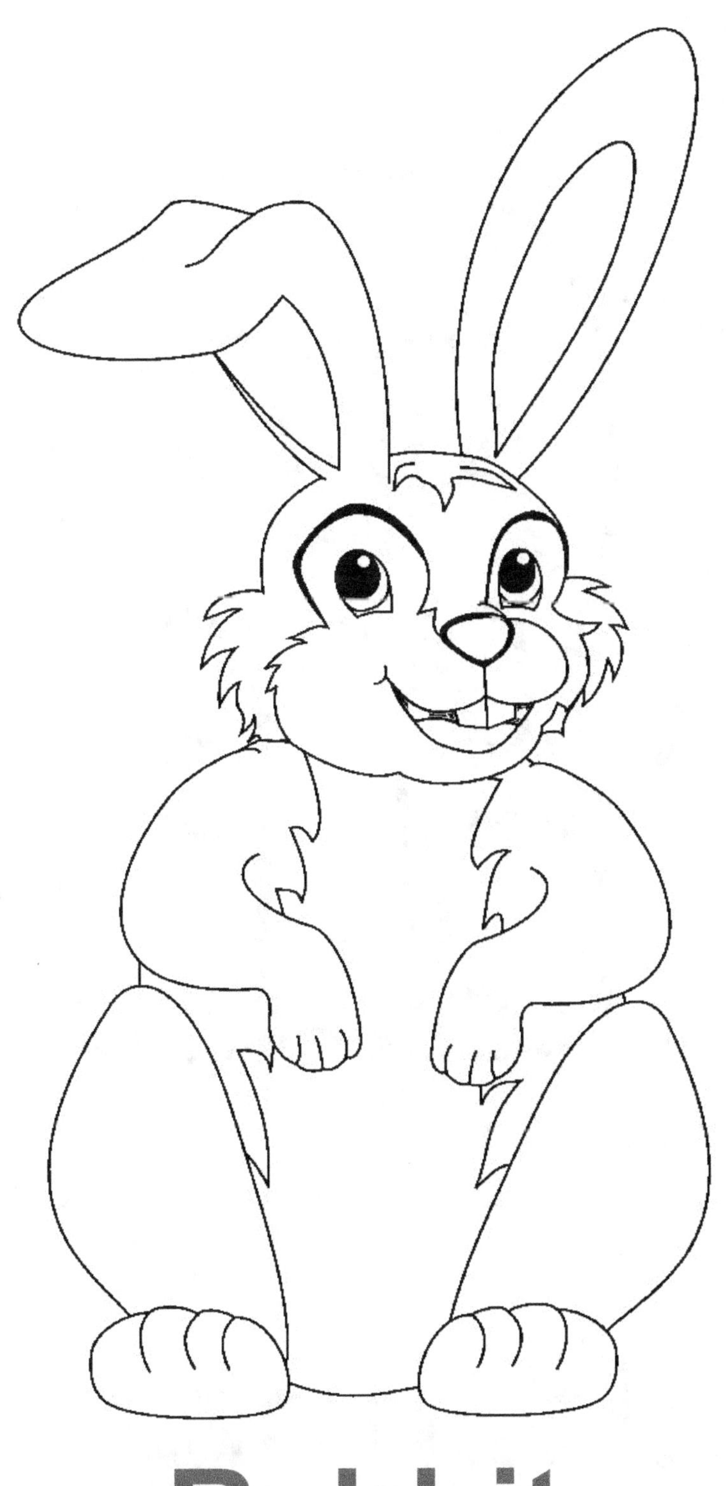

Rabbit

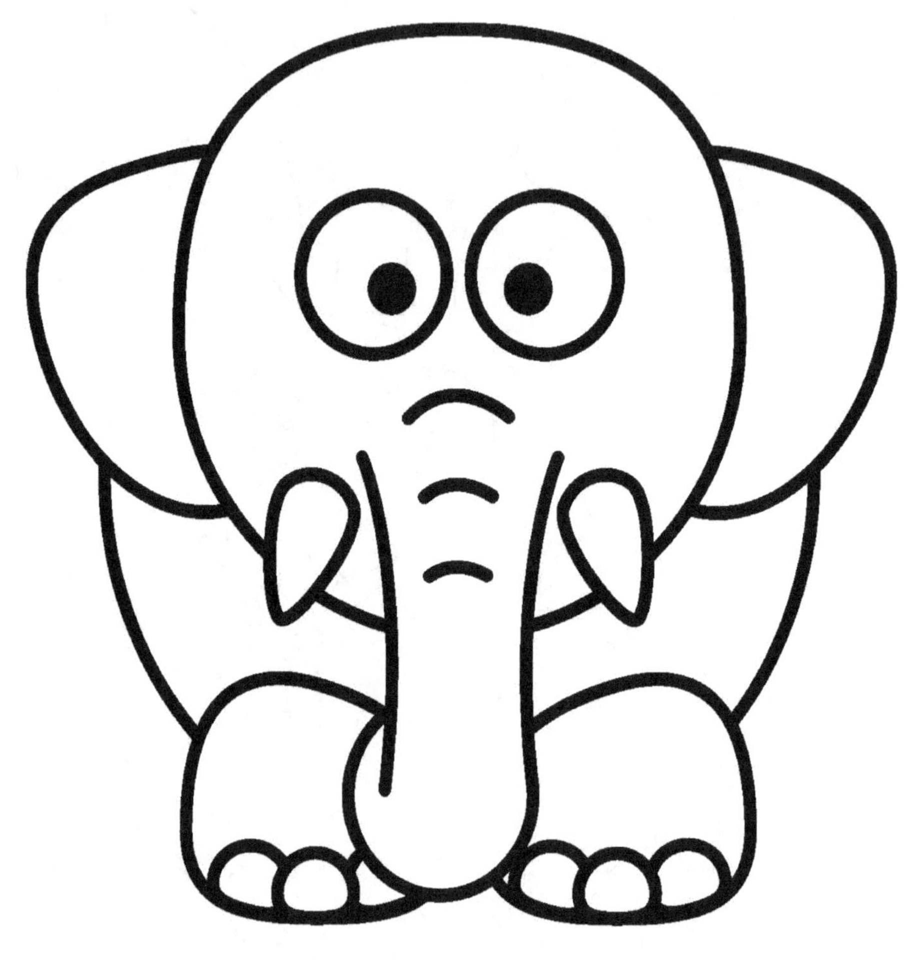

Elephant

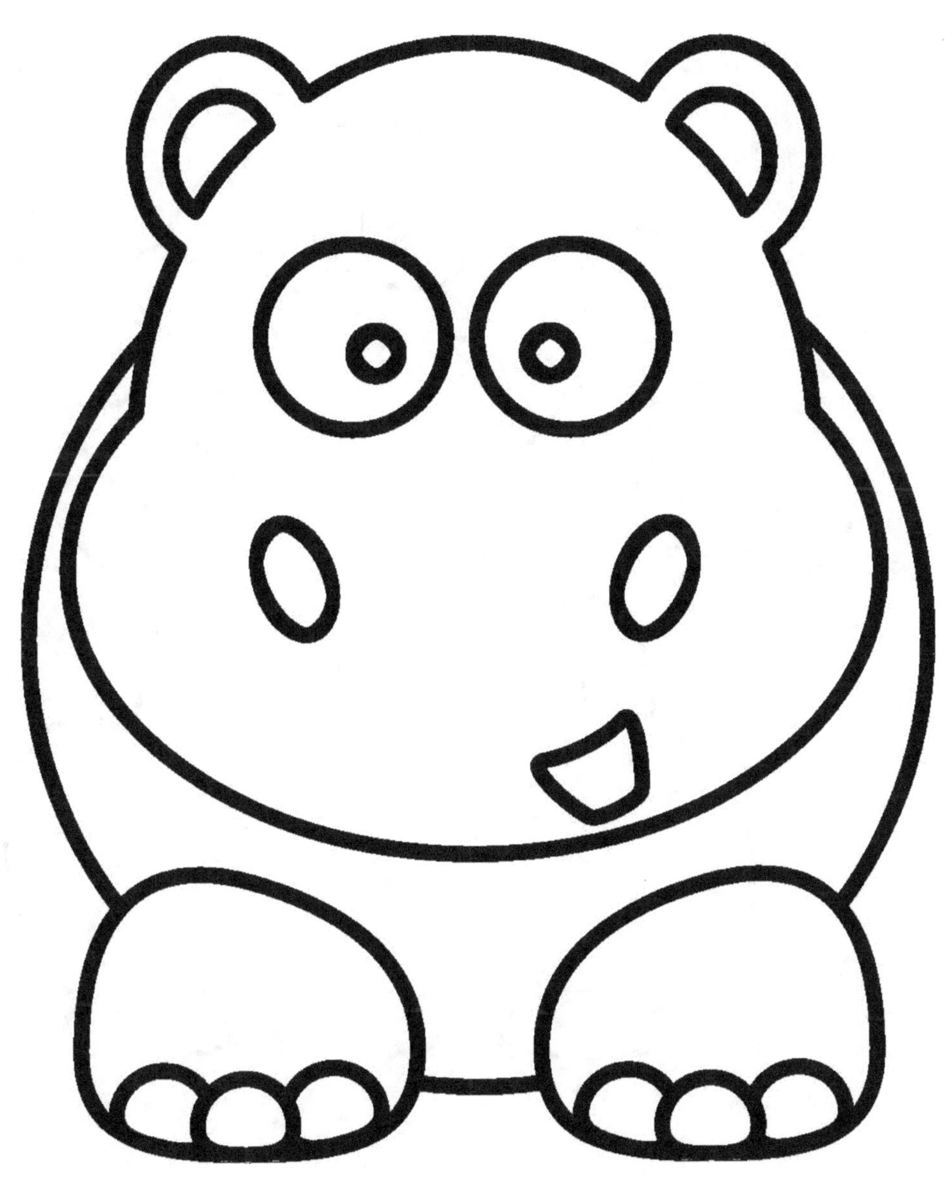

Hippopotamus

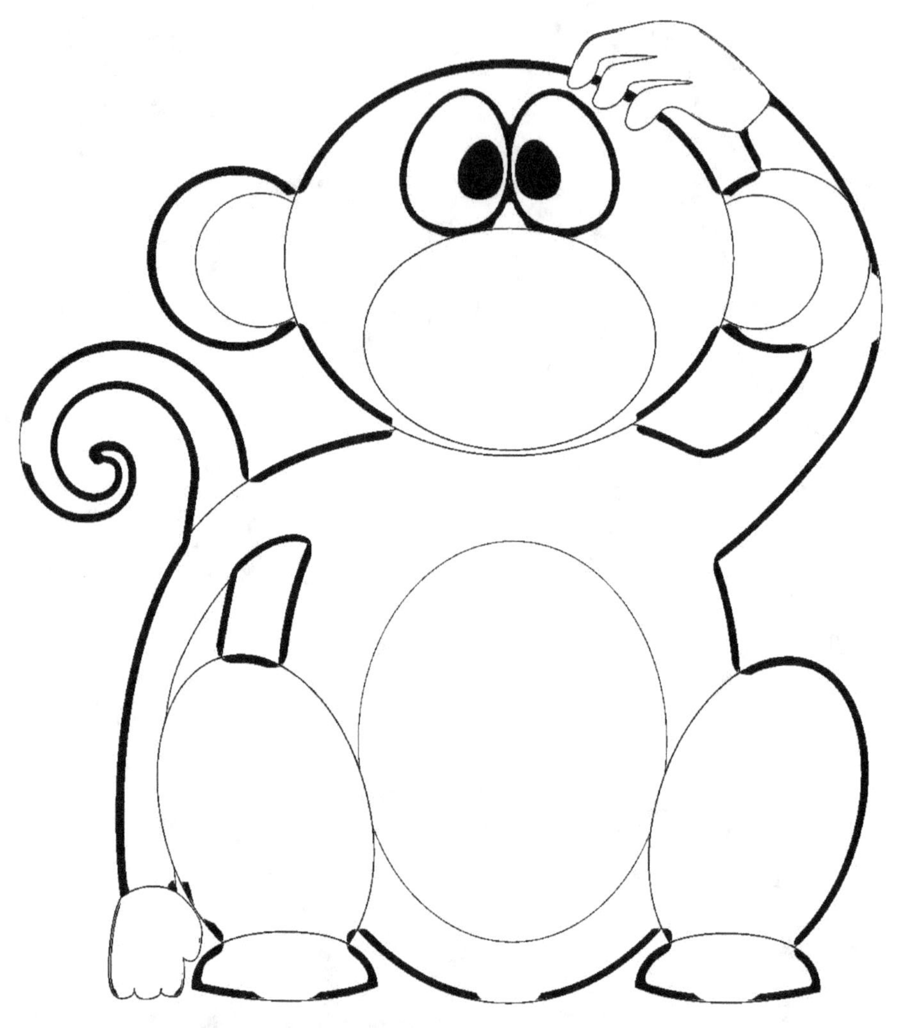

Monkey

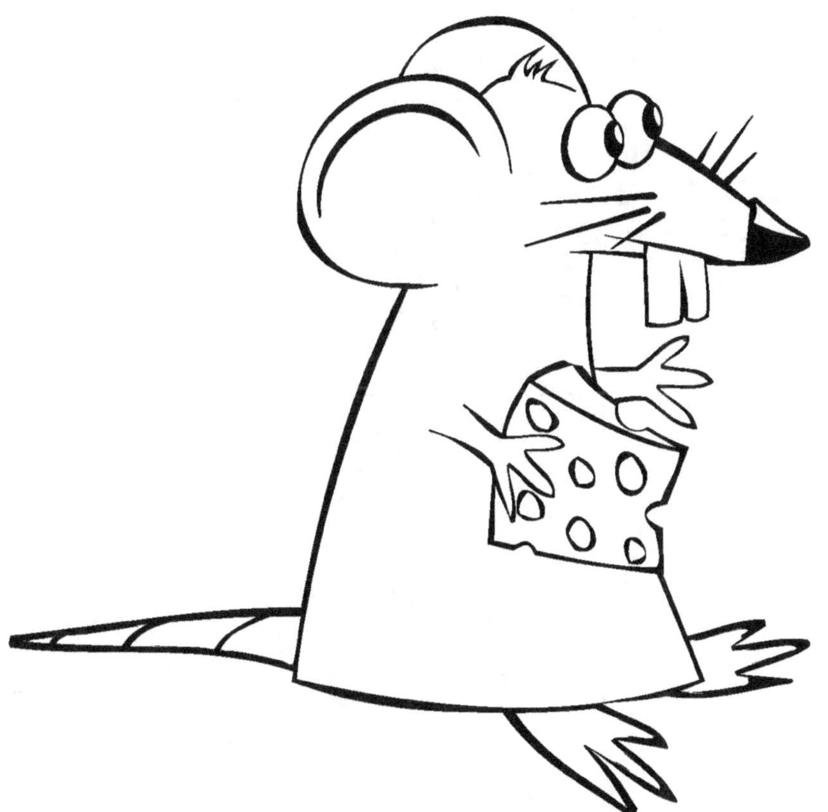

Mouse

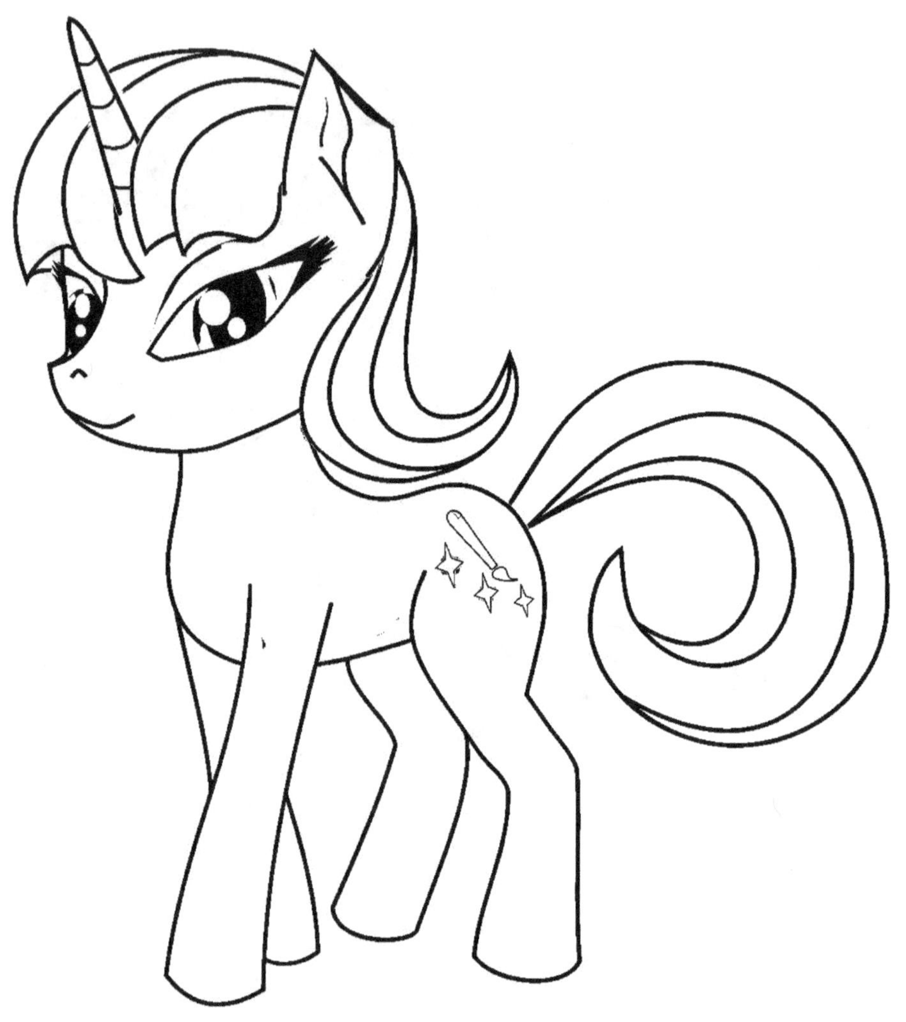

horse

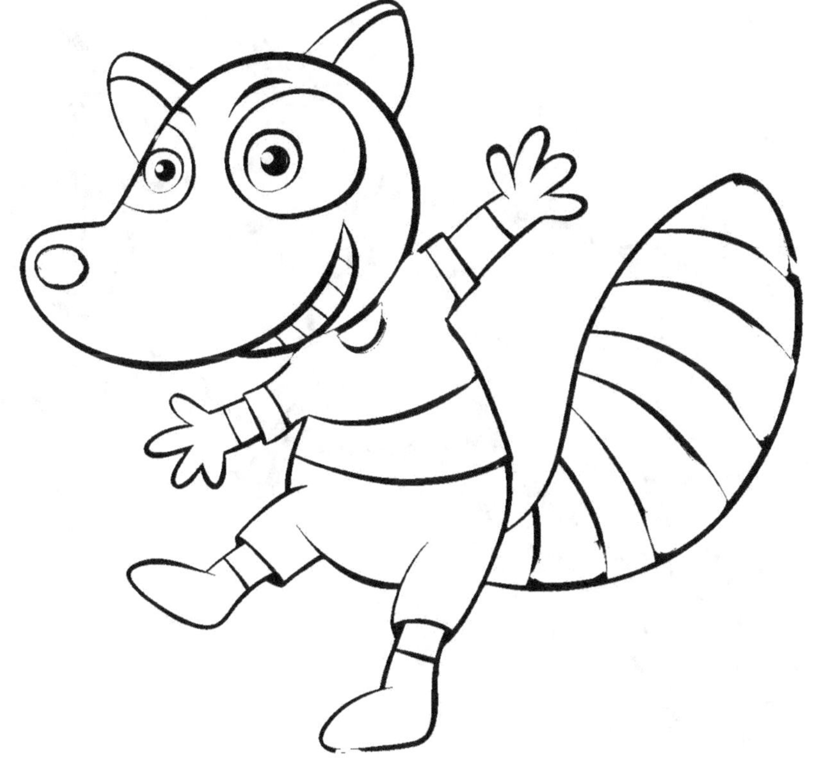

Beaver

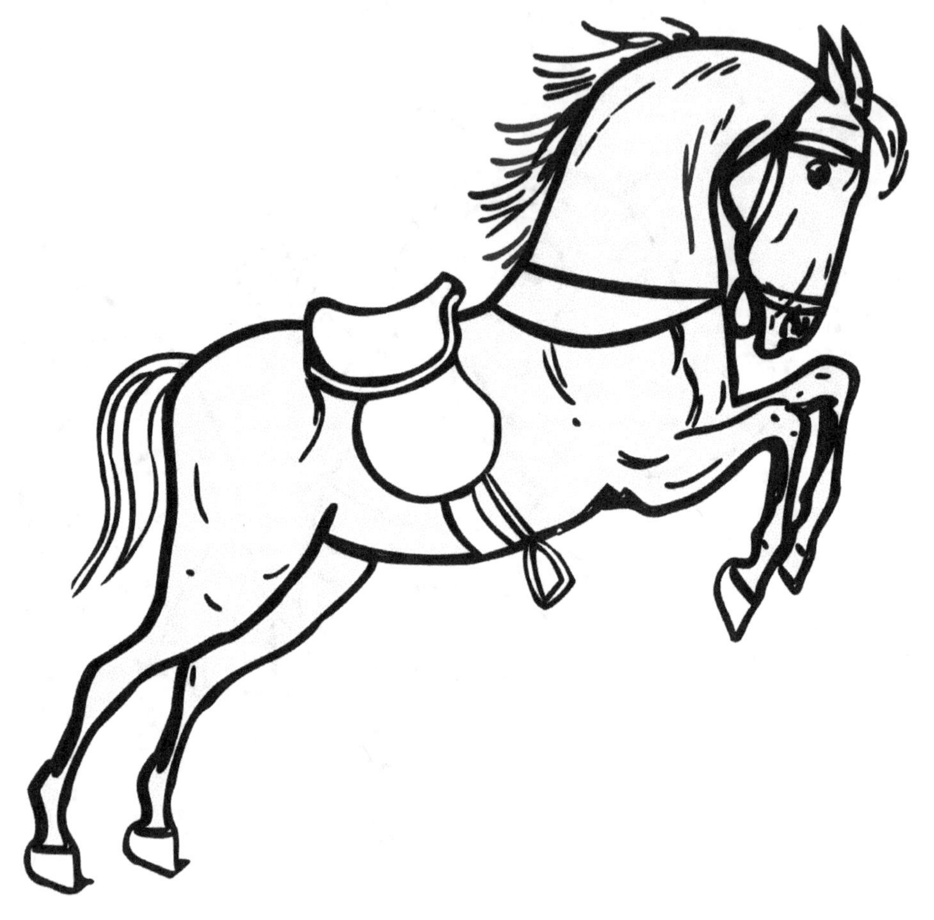

Horse

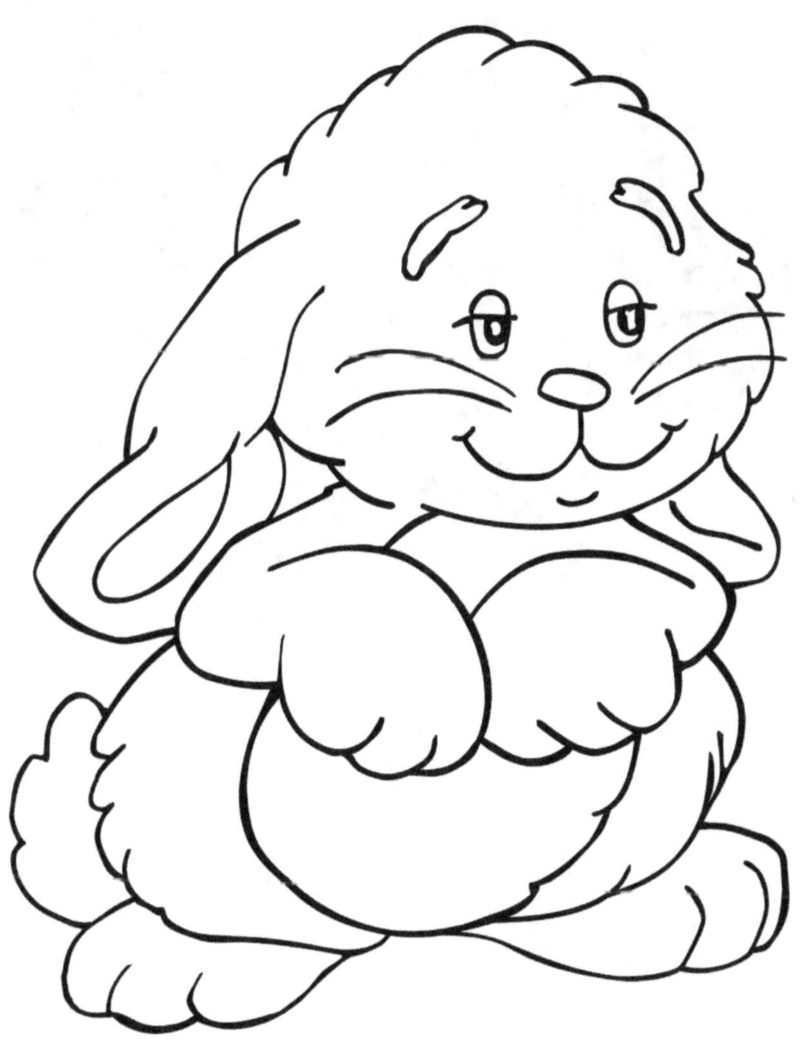

Rabbit

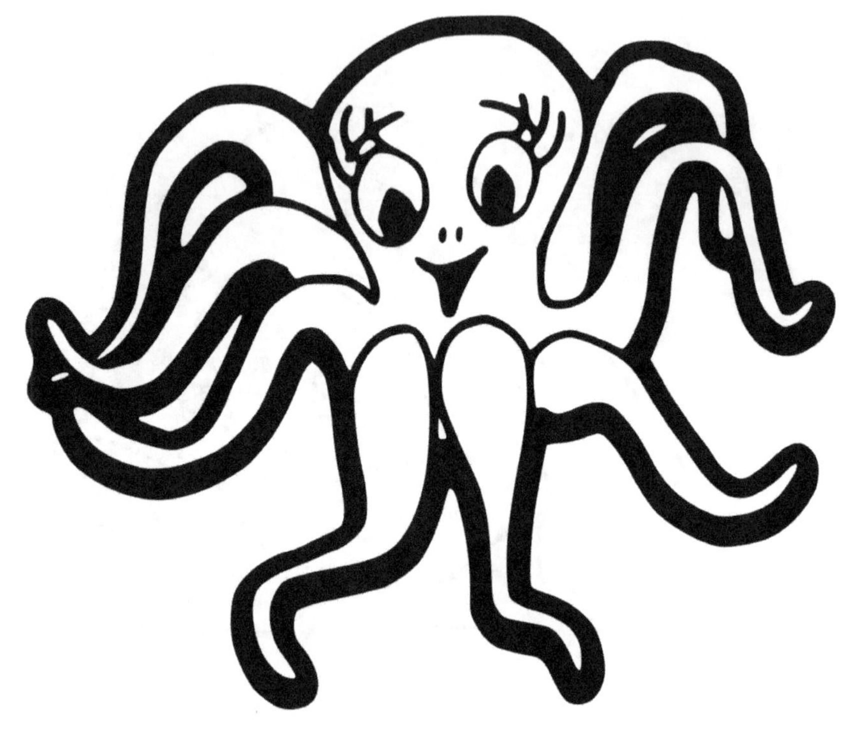

Octopus

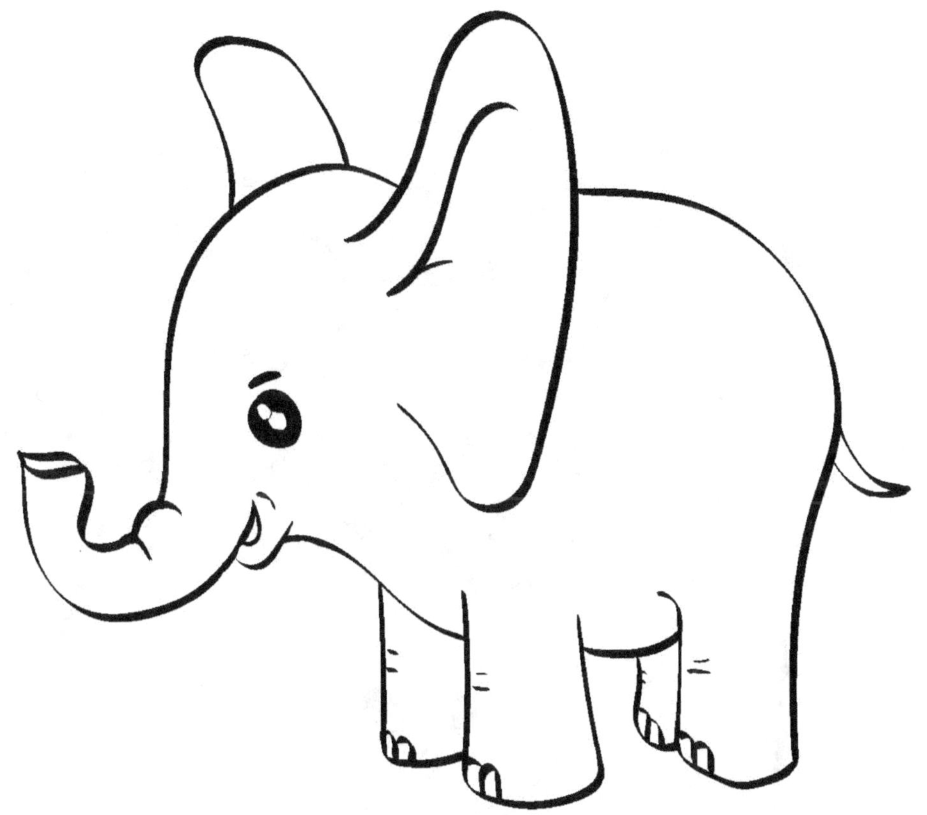

Elephant

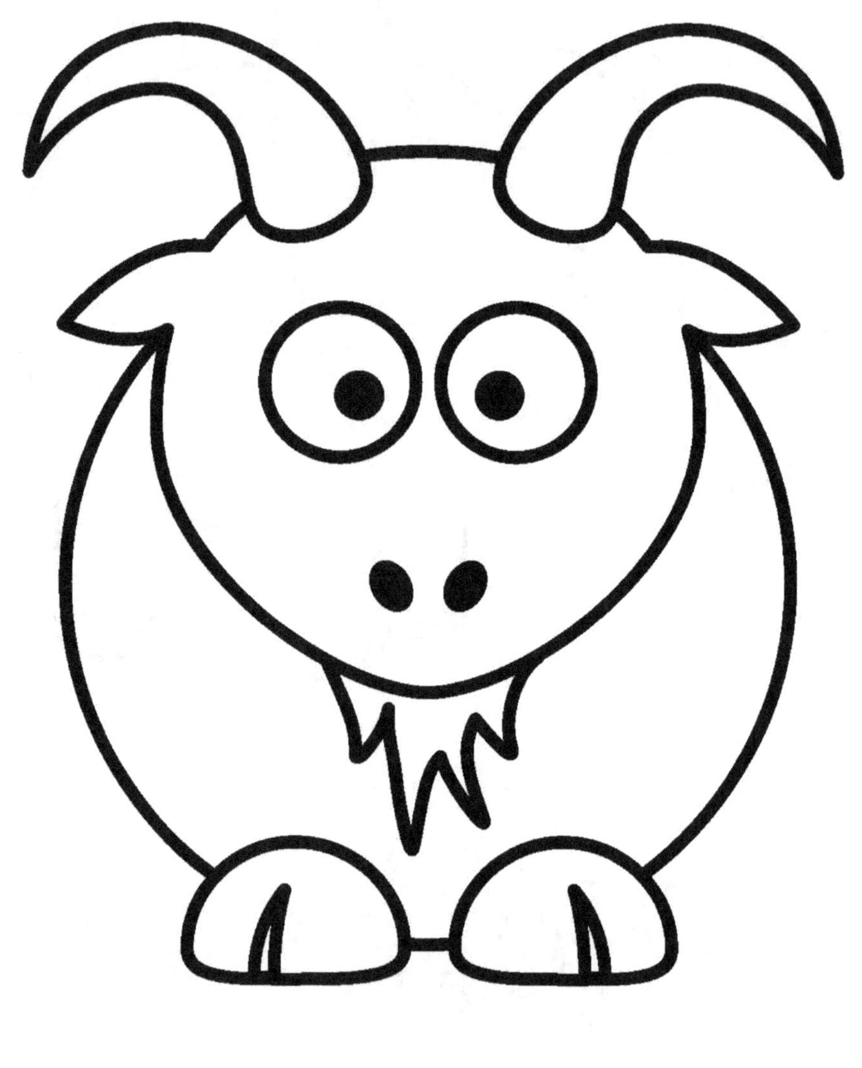

Goat

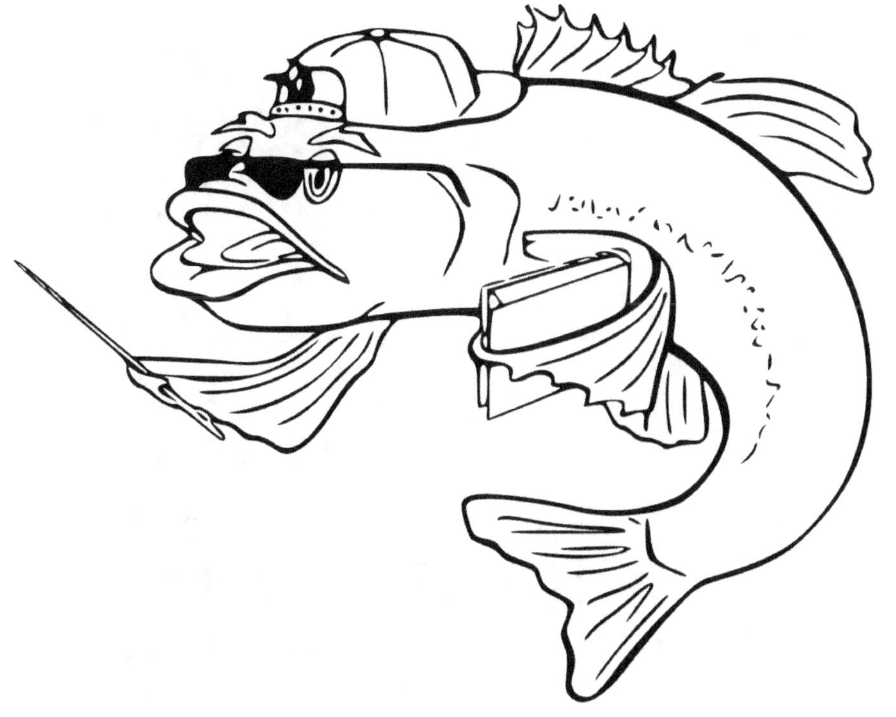

Fish

Contents